Scripted

just for You

a writing sourcebook

liz best

http://www.lizbest1.com, 2008

ISBN-13 978-0-9822519-0-4
ISBN-10 0-9822519-0-4

About the Author

Liz Best is a change agent. She is the founder and president of Best Writing & Consulting Services, Incorporated and the senior partner of its subsidiary, The Best Group.

She has provided keynote addresses and training for the private, business, faith-based and non-denominational organizations throughout the US, Canada and the Caribbean.

Her message is straight forward, "take a risk; you will grow from it." This book echoes that sentiment. It is bold and empowering.

Other published works by Liz Best include:

Embracing First-time Students: The Retention Model that Works, Gentle Persuasions and The CORE.

Acknowledgements

I thank God for blessing me with a creative gift and for my husband, Neville; for my sister, Josephine and for their consistent support and encouragement to live my dream through my work.

Table of Contents

Preface

Research has shown that open-minded people successfully birth creative ideas. They are risk takers whose imagination fuel diverse perspectives for empowerment. This unprecedented sourcebook provides creative practical writing strategies for individuals who want to have their work in print as self publishers. It illustrates how to structure book writing content that will lure and retain targeted readers. It also succinctly demonstrates the differences between wishful thinking, writing with a purpose, and getting published within a specific time frame.

The lure of this book is its introductory chapter. It is similar to foreplay in a romantic encounter. Foreplay is essential to an exciting and engaging activity designed to lure individuals with the expectancy of a more involved and exciting romantic experience.

The introductory title, His Lips Excite Me, is crafted to illustrate creativity, vivid imagination and taking some risk to write. It sets the tone for a very intriguing and exciting book writing experience and is reminiscent of a good appetizer before a fantastic meal. This chapter is designed to camouflage the actual book content. Readers will identify and grasp the pros and cons of focused writing in a very simplistic way.

The introduction has a deliberate sensual connotation with a predisposition to personal disclosure. Alarming as it may be, by the time readers would have completed reading this book, I can assure you that they will be pleasantly surprised.

Ghostwriters find it less appealing to rewrite and re-edit clients' work because of the additional time and costs that are incurred. It was labor intensive for me and very frustrating because my clients made simple mistakes and I wanted them to know the fundamentals of liberated and structured writing. Even though I had to charge them for the time spent, I was more committed to showing them how to do something that was very simplistic about their writing styles or habits.

Burdened by my desire to share some techniques, I offered and presented a one-day workshop entitled, "Write Your Own Book in 60 Days." It provided a great opportunity to demonstrate some writing strategies. I was able to share some value-added benefits of taking extreme liberty with their vocabulary to express their thoughts in writing. I was also able to illustrate how conservative thinking and a lack of writing structure inhibited written expression. These factors failed to convey a clear, interesting and succinct sentiment or message. They also significantly minimized book content and predictably accommodated writer's block. After that workshop experience, I yearned to equip prospective writers with some practical tools to use and quickly access as a reliable sourcebook.

I chose this title, to encourage and motivate those persons who lack confidence to unleash their vivid imagination and put their creative ideas in writing. This topic provides some very unique perspectives on creative and personally-explicit expressions. The creative illustration equips both new and experienced writers with tools to transition into a very powerful dimension in written communications.

After much contemplation, I realized that writing this introduction was the most valuable lesson in print that I could have shared to mobilize readers to maximize their vocabularies when they write. More importantly, research has shown that working adults need practical but conversational illustrations that are straightforward and easy to follow as self-publishers of different genres.

It is important to emphasize that there are three important words in this introductory chapter, His Lips Excite Me. Specifically, those words are "**lips, excite** and **me.**" They are the subject, verb and object of this sentence. Since the word, "his" is a pronoun, acting on behalf of a noun or the name like Tom, Dick or Harry for example, it is less important to focus on it for this writing illustration.

It is for this reason that most of what you will learn from this creative writing exercise, will evolve around different perspectives on "lips," "excite" and how those two words, impact or have some relationship to the word, "me."

The critical thing to observe is how many different situations, perspectives or activities will evolve around those words. Pay close attention to the movements, gestures and sentiments of his lips. Observe the specific situations regarding the who, what, where, when, why and how his lips excite me.

His Lips Excite Me

Most readers will probably want to know whose lips would excite me to such an extent that I have to write about them. I can only assume that readers may also be wondering whether those lips belong to my husband, a friend, my lover or whether they are all the same person.

Some curiosity may propel some readers to imagine what "he" may know or do to me so differently with his lips that would give me such excitement. I encourage you to read with an open mind so that you will better grasp the gravity of my excitement about his lips. You may be able to identify for yourself what kind of lips he has; what he does with them, how he does it, why he does it, when, and under what circumstances his lips excite me.

Wherever your imagination may take you, I thought I should caution you to consider the size and texture of his lips. In so doing, you may want to ask yourself a few of the following questions: Are his lips large, small, full, thin, nicely textured, soft and spongy, or are they so soft that they feel like plastic or a well-worked over piece of chewing gum?

What if they were very chapped or cracked by the wind simply because he lives and works in a warm, dry or cold climate? Do you think his lips might be discolored from smoking or from his terrible pencil-biting habits when he is in deep concentration? Can you imagine what his lips may look like during any of those times to really excite me? What if they were parched from his incessant drinking of harsh alcoholic beverages? But read on. It gets a little more interesting.

There is an old cliché that says, "Curiosity kills the cat," so whatever you do, try to follow this story line, "lips excite me." Go with the flow of the information shared and refrain from getting too carried away with any situational inferences or peculiar descriptions of his lips. I would encourage you to keep your imagination in harness for just a moment.

It may not be too good of an idea to speculate on how his lips might be positioned on his face. The reason is that he moves his lips around often depending on his moods or motives. Maybe you are more curious to find out whether his lips are proportionately or disproportionately sized to his pointed, flat, round or crooked nose. What if his lips were crowned neatly with a well-groomed, curled-up-at-the-end moustache of sandy blonde, dark brown or black hair which allows his teeth to look freshly brushed and attractive?

Perhaps he has no hair on his upper lip. Can you just imagine what his lips would look like if they were parked above some pearly white, coffee-stained or absent teeth? Do you think I could get excited about his teeth if they were cavity-ridden? Or do you think the absence of his teeth has cast such a dark shadow in his mouth that when he laughs it reminds me of some cozy romantic or hideous place in my distant past?

Maybe his lips excite me because they mimic and release the sound of a hollow tunnel when he speaks because of his loose-fitting dentures. Quite frankly, one of the things that I get excited by is the semi-circular shape of his lips as he shifts from simple conversation to hearty laughter. Because of his various facial expressions, I am comfortable disclosing how he smacks his lips after he eats a delicious meal. Those smacking sounds remind me of a poorly-strung musical instrument from last year's band. These sounds seem to bewail and beckon for help from its bandmaster. His lips are something different to listen to when he is in that lip-smacking mode and much funnier to look at. His smacking lips embarrass me but make me giddy with laughter because of how quickly he recovers from a foolish-looking child to a respectable intelligent adult with his facial expressions.

It is truly amazing to observe the nuances in his facial expressions and the dominant role his lips play on his face. His expressions sometimes range from an innocent angel, a mischievous lost lad waiting to be rescued, to a hungry hunk waiting for its prey.

Some (heterosexual) women may find their significant male friends' lips more interesting or attractive if their lips had a stub of hair below their bottom lips, a pencil-lined patch of hair above their top lips, or a "goatee" on their chins that may announce over-stated masculinity.

Whatever excites women about their significant male persons' lips is very personal. Because of our unique personal preferences, I am comfortable sharing these sentiments... weird as they may seem. On the other hand, I would be remiss if I did not acknowledge that men have similar preferences to appreciate the impact of their significant females' personal attributes or styles. Some men may prefer a certain shade of lipstick or lip gloss that women wear or might just appreciate seeing their naked lips with a hint of lip gloss. I hope you understand how personal preferences dictate excitement in different people.

Wherever your imagination allows you to travel as you try to determine how his lips excite me, please stay focused. Try not to get too ahead of yourself with excitement as I sometimes do. I am only talking about his lips and not his tongue. We all know that the human tongue is known to tickle. It literally "tickles your fancy" (as in humor) or wherever it may gently touch. The tongue is also known to be troublesome, primarily because of its involvement in some inappropriate or premature bantering conversations.

The Bible underscores a similar sentiment about the tongue and warns us that "the tongue is a deadly weapon which is hard to harness." Because of these nuances in which the tongue can be a serious distraction, it would be wise to keep the sentiment of how his lips excite me separately from that of his tongue, and in its proper perspective.

Sometimes my excitement is heightened by the way he would wryly smile just before he does something naughty. Can you imagine what pleasure that mischievous smile brings me when I think about his expression on a gloomy day especially when he is not around me? When I am alone and realize how he tries to test my patience by symmetrically winking his right eye and strangely twisting both of his lips like the shape of a broken zipper, I get really excited and indulge in a real chuckle. I have come to realize that this is his way of letting me know that he is about to "pluck my nerves."

However, instead of buying into the trap that he orchestrates to provoke me, I have also learned to pensively observe his best efforts and smile with anticipation for him to entertain me since I am now capable of reading his lips. I know when he is setting me up as he postures for a healthy debate. However, I find his lips to be less exciting during these times because they are about to get a bit loose and somewhat uncomfortable for me to appreciate.

When they get loose, they are capable of uttering insignificant words and sentiments that are similar to an introduction of an unnecessary argument. This posturing sentiment of his, conjures up the idea similar to someone having diarrhea of the lips. At this point, all I can honestly do is to totally ignore him because I do not know what might trickle out of his lips. Since I am not disposed to readily filtering garbage through my ear for it to take residence in my head without paying rent, or a price for it, I vacate his space.

Recognizing that he has struck a nerve with me, he turns up his lips like a clown and says something radically hilarious. But that's not all. He complements this expression with as wide a smile as you can ever imagine that simply melts my heart. Invariably this puts a very reluctant smile on my face.

Can you imagine a pair of lips looking like a half moon with a twinkling star parked in the corner of someone's mouth? His lips sometimes convey that expression. It is truly a beautiful sight to behold! Even though his conversations may be very provoking at times, his accompanying smile and subsequent laughter propel me to pay close attention to every word that trickles out of his mouth. I get excited watching him perform. I chose the word trickle to emphasize the drama that comes from his lips as he speaks. His words seem to be very carefully orchestrated to humor or appease me because he has such a way of getting me excited and transforming my moods. Anyone observing that transformation would think I am in love; have been smitten by some magic wand; have been stung by a mysterious bug of some sort, or might have lost my mind. The contrast in my personality is like day and night as he charms me with his lips.

For the most part, his lips do have some alluring qualities with extraordinary expressions. They excite me when he eats soft ice-cream and laps up every lingering drip like a thirsty lost puppy. The more he laps them up, the plumper his lips seem to become. His lips are simply amazing to watch when they change texture and color. Can you imagine him trying to arrest and devour every drip of ice cream? His facial expressions travel from a thirsty lost puppy to a seemingly half-starved little child. There is no shame in his game!

But here is the most amazing thing. When he finishes his ice-cream and returns to full-blown adulthood, he positions himself to demonstrate his three-dimensional kisses on me. Quite frankly, I never realized that there could be enough room on anyone's lower lip to accommodate three kisses in three different places without saliva overflow. There is absolutely no dribble in this drama! He claims that his kisses express the true sentiments of his heart. I sincerely hope that you can understand the excitement I experience from the contrasting things that he does with his lips to derail and excite me.

If you are honest with yourself, you would realize that such an affectionate expression could cause anyone to have "additional" mood swings (because we all have them). They would melt your heart, and cause you to feel special or more valued as a mate, particularly in the absence of bad breath.

Sometimes, the weird gestures of his lips become particularly overbearing when he insists on getting my undivided attention. When I ignore him, he has this habit of puckering his lips, tilting his head to the right at a 45-degree angle, winking his right eye and blowing me gentle kisses. If I fall for these gestures of affection without consciously thinking about how cleverly he orchestrates his attention-getting plan, I could easily get sucked right into them like a tornado preceding a very dangerous hurricane.

One of his favorite gestures is to physically enter and crowd my space. He then places his lips close to my check, never touching my face and mimics imaginary kisses. His little absent pecks on my cheek, convey the sentiment, "I am not giving up. I'll be b-a-c-k!" His lips really do excite me when he acts like this. I feel vulnerable like a lamb before its slaughter, helpless and dumbfounded when he teases me like this. It is at this point that I recognize that there is a price tag for everything in life, even at this level of excitement. He is so very smooth with his "game plan" that I sometimes find it very easy to forget that he has ulterior motives.

I am sure that his familiarity with me propels him to take more liberties than I am sometimes willing to accommodate. The more I think about his lips, the more I feel compelled to ask... what would you do if you were caught between the gentle whispers of your significant person's lips and the sentimental gestures of his or her personal affection? Isn't it exciting?

What would you do if for some strange reason, you found that the sentimental gestures and gentle whispers of your significant person's lips, invariably had the capacity to respond to your unexpressed needs or steer you in the right direction particularly when you least expected? Is that exciting or what? Would you call that love, real kinship, togetherness or as my pastor, Rev. Jamal Bryant, would say, a true sign of "with-ness" (the synchronized thought processes of two people who are closely and emotionally connected)?" When I experienced that particular situation, I was tempted to think that he was clairvoyant. But it was most exciting because I did not realize that his lips had that kind of impact on my life or how closely we were connected.

In spite of how I may interpret what happens to me when his lips get in my face or the memory of his warm affection, I have learned to cherish and look forward to those specially- exciting moments. I feel especially blessed because I could have been bored with a barren desire for affection from a significant male person. If I did not experience such excitement, I also could have resided in a constant state of anxiety, waiting to exhale without the comfort of such fond memories. It may seem like a crazy sentiment but it is truly wonderful to experience and share how his lips excite me.

As Shakespeare puts it, "it is better to have loved and lost than never to have loved at all." Whether it is love or heavy excitement, you will define it for yourself once you have experienced what I have shared. Just hang in there. Your day is coming!

By now, I can imagine that you are probably anxious and ready to learn whose lips excite me. I could also assume that you are probably sitting on the edge of your chair waiting to find out from where does my greatest excitement from his lips come. Quite honestly, I am somewhat torn between what his lips look like when he frames his words to speak and when he laughs heartily. I really have not made up my mind which one of those two situations excite me more.

The reason for my ambivalence is that on the one hand when he speaks, it is usually about something very profound or funny. When he laughs, he has a very innocent and alluring countenance because of how widely he spreads his lips and exposes his teeth. However, there is something very exciting to me about that latter sentiment.

If you expected or were trying to figure out something more romantically explicit about how his lips might have excited me, I regret disappointing you. Those two situations do it for me. I admit that his lips are very exciting to me but his unique facial expressions lure and take me to a comfortable and emotionally different place most of the time. I am absolutely sure about that! You can call me weird if you like, but that's it!

The situational references I have shared so far about how his lips excite me, were reflective of some very personal moments I might have experienced. The lure of what he does with his lips tends to introduce me to something more exciting. This type of foreplay is most significant to me because I really never know what he may do with his lips to engage, educate, entertain, humor or excite me. I am always in awe of him. He is affectionate, funny, intelligent, and mischievous and his lips tell unpredictable different stories at different times.

Has your curiosity gotten the best of you yet as you try to determine what else he does with his lips to excite me that I will share? As you may recall, my intention was to have you salivate for what you will find out on the following pages of this book. Are you frustrated about my non-disclosure yet? If you are yearning to find out something more exciting about the excitement of his lips, I would suggest that you reflect on the sentiments that I have shared about writing with vivid imagination and creativity. There is some method to my non-disclosure of who he is and you should have cultivated some appreciation for how I have tried to engage you thus far.

You will notice that I have placed heavy emphasis on the excitement of his lips with bold creativity and vivid imagination. Have you realized how much one can write about a simple subject? In this case, it is the word, "lips." In the title, His lips excite me, the verb or action word, "excite" has propelled me to creatively think of every possible thing or situation about what the subject, "lips" can do, looks like or where it is positioned to say the least. Would you ever believe that a simple subject like "lips" would generate such creativity or send my thought processes in so many different directions? If you simply unleash and let your imagination go wild, you will do wonders with your topic.

As risky as this introductory topic and this creative writing journey have been, I have taken into account the sentiments of personal disclosure. To disclose the person whose lips excite me, would defeat my purpose for writing this introductory chapter in this manner. The lesson to be learned here is to let go and let your creative imagination take you on the journey to express yourself.

While disclosure of who he is, might be important to you, a cursory review of the personal sentiments of affection I have shared, obviously leave room for unanswered questions. However, it was not my intention to create more curiosity for you to ask some in-depth questions, conjure up ideas for which I am not prepared to answer or deal with. I have no desire to have you hold me hostage to those sentiments of affection about how his lips excite me. Instead, I would like you to examine the pattern of non-disclosure which I have creatively shared. It is important to recognize the lure, ambiguity and intrigue of this subject matter, "lips." So I acquiesce.

This introduction was designed to emphasize the

importance of being task-focused on the identified subject, "lips." This illustration should encourage you to be very descriptive and graphic when expressing your personal thoughts in writing… whether they are true or false. It is also important to recognize the contrast of this introductory chapter to the core content of this book as you read on.

Rest assured that your words and creative writing skills will take on a new and different life of their very own after you would have read this book. I hope that you will understand my intended purpose and be forgiving of my non-disclosure. Even though I took you on this creative writing journey, this lesson does have merit. You will be better off for taking the trip.

I know from experience that the topic of writing is not as fascinating to read about for many busy adults. They want to get to the heart of the "dos and don'ts" of writing in a hurry. Most working adults want to get critical writing information without taking time to learn fundamental principles or objectively identify what they need to do to get to where they want to be. However, writing with greater impact is a process.

I am sensitive to the behavior of many busy working adults so I chose to anticipate and respond to those needs by constructing these writing essentials to accommodate that purpose.

The information that you will find on the following pages will help persons who have the desire to improve their writing skills. It will objectively structure and support writing ideas succinctly. Prospective self-publishers with exciting ideas will benefit greatly from the bulleted information via guidelines and strategies. The writing processes will systematically and comfortably facilitate the writing process to release your thoughts freely, clearly and confidently.

As long as one identifies a topic or subject on which he or she wants to write, he or she will exit this book with a greater grasp on how diverse, descriptive and mysterious he or she can write. Their experience or thoughts will propel them to write more creatively. I truly believe that if a person can conceive of something, he or she can definitely write well on the subject.

For those of you who might still be concerned about whether his lips excite me is true or false, who he is or whether it is my overactive imagination, I suggest that you put all those concerns to rest. If you are still unsure and curious, then my illustration to graphically punctuate the importance of luring and maintaining your readers' interests was successful.

By the time you would have read this book, you will also learn how to be less conservative with your vocabulary. You would be more confident to follow your intuition; indulge your creativity to expand upon your vocabulary and write with great passion and conviction. You should no longer be like those very articulate people who suppress their vocabulary; minimize their ideas and refuse to punctuate their deepest thoughts with passion when they write. This sourcebook is designed to relieve you of those behaviors.

The core content of this book includes abbreviated guidelines and strategies to simplify the writing process for many writers. It does not comprehensively image strategies for technical or scholarly publications. These guidelines are simplistic and straightforward. They accommodate working adults who are comfortable with refreshing and adhering to simplistic writing structures. This reader-friendly sourcebook is practical for people with busy lifestyles. It gets to the heart of information for fiction and non-fiction writing genres.

As a responsible married woman, I chose the introductory chapter and content because I know a "little something" about the subject. The nuances in which his lips excite me that I have described, could have preceded or do currently exist in my marriage of almost 24 years. The underlying premise and relevance of this topic," his lips excite" evolve around creativity, experience, vivid imagination, risk, passion and vocabulary expression. These perspectives help to punctuate this topic in different ways.

When writers understand the benefits of pungently expressing themselves from all of those perspectives in writing, it boosts their confidence and improves their writing skills. It is essential to incorporate the fundamentals of good grammar, an open mind, risk, discipline and patience to fuel book writing content. Using a marketability mindset to structure book content should complement the writing process.

One of the critical things a writer has to do is to set his or her imagination free to engage a wide range of readers. This requires some risks. Being verbally expressive unravels the cobwebs that clog creativity. Liberating your mind expedites the book-writing process to provide greater content and clarity.

The illustrated strategies and guidelines give excellent wiggle room for rewriting and editing. The bulleted summaries set the tone for more focused writing on a variety of genres. They illustrate what to do to quickly capture and retain the readers' interests in a very structured and succinct manner. They also significantly assist those persons who already have ideas about what types of books they want to write.

When these formatted guidelines are modeled, any fear of writing is conquered. Organizing one's thoughts help to engage diverse readers' interest. These steps provide greater insight about your own writing capacity to stay focused and meet your identified writing goals, objectives and most importantly, your real deadlines.

As you examine and practice these exercises, remember to write about something with which you are thoroughly familiar. It will help you to write with passion and conviction. Writing requires commitment and discipline. Persons who are not disciplined or are afraid of structure, this book format will show you how to become disciplined, relaxed and comfortable with the bulleted strategies which are less intimidating to follow. So read with an open mind. Be empowered and get published!

NOTES

Some things I must do now are:

1. _____

2. _____

3. _____

4. _____

5. _____

6. _____

7. _____

8. _____

9. _____

10. _____

11. _____

12. _____

13. _____

14. _____

15. _____

Organizing Your Thoughts

This sourcebook provides information for the following genres: fiction, non-fiction, autobiography, poetry, children's books and short stories. In an attempt to maximize the content of this book and attract a very diverse group of readers, I have identified six very important questions for you to consider. To organize your thoughts well, it is important to be very clear about what type of book you will be writing and whether it is fiction or non-fiction.

Identifying the type of writing genre helps to shape the content of your book and serves to lay a foundation for everything you will need to write about on the topic of your choice. Organizing your thoughts provides clarity to express your ideas and reinforce your book content.

As you review the following introspective questions for your particular writing project, understand that they are randomly selected primarily because writers may be at different stages in their writing process. However, from a realistic perspective, you would need to ask yourself the following questions if you are truly serious about writing. It is important to have some incentive, be motivated and committed to getting your book published in the not-too-distant future with a specific deadline. The questions you may need to ask yourself are as follows:

1. Am I overwhelmed by the possible cost to write, publish edit, print, market or promote my book?

2. Do book royalties concern me?

3. Am I only day dreaming about writing my book, stuck writing one, ran out of content or am I almost finished?

4. Why do I want to write?

5. Am I writing to inform, motivate, persuade or educate?

6. What do I think readers want to walk away with after reading my book?

If you can unequivocally answer most of these questions with a resounding "yes or no" response, you are half way there. Once you have honestly answered these questions, you should list three reasons why you chose the topic or subject of your book. This will give you a solid foundation or platform for getting started. It will also clarify your purpose and identify what next steps are required for your unique type of writing.

It is a realistic practice to identify three persons or organizations that would buy your book and read it after you have completed it. This identification will remind you that your book should be written realistically for marketability.

The answers you get from the following questions should also propel you to streamline your thoughts and show you how much more research might be needed. As you begin to write, some other types of introspection should take place and some of your questions ought to include:

1. How do I plan to get the information or content to complete my book?

2. Should the sources of information that I need for my book come from primary research (self), surveys, the library or the internet?

3. When, exactly (what time of day) should I attempt to start writing my book?

The answer to question number three (3) requires that you seriously consider what time of the day that you are most productive, creative and are highly energized. For example, early in the morning, high noon, after a large meal, at night or before you go to bed, should be some of your real considerations. This is very important because it will identify your peak performance and creativity time.

4. Where should I attempt to write?

This question refers to the place or location of your writing site. If your home or office is not conducive to quietness where you can think clearly and creatively, you will have to identify a place that is void of distraction, very conducive to writing, creativity and relaxation.

5. How can I create my book outline or chapters?

This question is easy if you already know what you want to write about. It should also help you to recognize whether you have enough information or whether you have done enough research on the subject of your writing. If you have enough information for your content, then you can create an outline to establish some chapters.

The most effective way I have found to prepare an outline and develop chapters is to create a thesis statement for each topic/chapter of your book in a concise manner. A thesis statement is also referred to as a topic sentence.

After you have developed your thesis statements, list those sentences in some kind of order: chronological (ascending or descending), historical, by events or activities. This will help you to stay better organized and more focused on your topic.

Whatever you do, structure a beginning, middle and ending to every topic sentence. However, you should consider prioritizing your content sequentially in the same manner as you would, if you were going to build something where certain steps had to be done in sequence.

A good example of this is to envision that you are building a house where the foundation is laid before the rooms are built or if you are baking a cake where the flour is placed in the batter before it goes into the oven. As simplistic as this exercise may seem, writing will be just as easy if you would follow these structures.

The beginning sentence of your story idea should announce the content. The middle sentence embellishes a little on the introductory sentence and provides more substance to your story. It should begin with a thesis statement that introduces a specific and different topic. The ending sentence follows the basic pattern of your middle sentence with a slight introduction or continuation of that sentence. It leads you into the ending sentence or ending part of your story. Most of the time the end of your story provides a summary of all the parts or an overview of the entire content of the book.

After you would have processed this information and answered the following questions honestly, you will need to prioritize your book content. In doing so, you will clearly identify how to get and structure the information for your book that is lodged in your head.

Your responses to the questions below should facilitate your writing purpose with great ease:

1. Do I have an accessible working computer?

2. Can I type at a rate that allows me to unleash my ideas as fluidly as I can think about them? If I cannot type, do I have access to the appropriate writing software or someone to type for me?

3. What are some of the immediate distractions that I may encounter in the space or location in which I decide to use for writing my book?

4. Are there any small children, four-legged animals, a needy husband, wife or relative who may cause some distraction once I get started? If so, what can I do about that?

5. Do I have enough quality time for writing or some "me time" to concentrate or stay focused?

6. Does my current work schedule or lack of writing skills (basic word construction) restrict me from writing? If so, how and when?

7. Do I need help with my general book design or layout, editing sentence structure, or proofreading to gauge my progress and feel successful?

8. Can I find a second set of eyes to help me read what I write to give me good and objective feedback in a timely fashion?

9. How soon do I think I can start writing my book after

all considerations or questions have been answered?

10. Do I have a "drop-dead" date to finish my book?

Once you have honestly answered these questions, it is your responsibility to think of other situations that may restrict you from starting or completely writing your book within the time frame you have identified. You may want to solicit some professional help to assist you at any stage of your book writing process so that you can stay focused and on your identified schedule. The critical thing is that you are honest with yourself.

Based upon your personal assessment of your writing project and commitment, you will feel empowered and confident to get started. You will be relieved to discern what your real writing capacity is for completing your book and in what areas you may need help. You may even realize that you might have to pay for some of those technical writing, editing or book consulting services or postpone the entire writing idea.

It is a good idea to shop around for the best prices for the specific services you may need. You may contact me via my website, www.lizbest1.com if you need some help with this.

To ensure your writing commitment and alleviate any apprehension about writing, incorporate and post the following "Writing Affirmations" which will keep you on schedule.   Posting them in a prominent place will remind and motivate you daily of your writing objective or project. Be sure to revisit them often because consistency and perseverance are the keys for seeing your writing project come to fruition.

NOTES

Some things I must do now are:

1. _____

2. _____

3. _____

4. _____

5. _____

6. _____

7. _____

8. _____

9. _____

10. _____

11. _____

12. _____

13. _____

14. _____

15. _____

Writing Affirmations

The following writing affirmations are designed to keep you focused on your commitment. They will reinforce and ensure that you are serious about your writing project. You should have them accessible for you to repeat or read aloud if you are in anyway distracted from your writing purpose.

1. I pledge to finish my book this year.

    (Place the date here_____).

2. I will turn off my TV and hide the remote.

3. I will meditate, pray and find a quiet or inspirational place in which I can write and be productive.

4. I will create a writing schedule because I am on a special assignment.

5. I will follow my Writing Activity Schedule.

6. I will follow the writing guidelines and tips for writing my book.

7. I will write at least four (4) pages a day and take two (2) days off a week to relax and be rejuvenated.

8. I will inform family members and friends of my commitment to finish my book and within the designated timeframe I have identified.

9. I will read and review similar books and their specific segments like: paragraphs, beginning, middle and ending for content comparison and structure.

10. I will proofread, edit and reread my manuscript before sending my book to the publisher.

NOTES

Some things I must do now are:

1. _____

2. _____

3. _____

4. _____

5. _____

6. _____

7. _____

8. _____

9. _____

10. _____

11. _____

12. _____

13. _____

14. _____

15. _____

Your Targeted Readers

One's perception of writing and the reality to get through this process will improve with practice, commitment and an open mind. Perceptions about writing change and publishing dreams come through when commitment is acknowledged and reinforced.

To capture and retain your targeted readers' interests, you may want to visualize that you have an intense problem and can resolve it independently and objectively. This exercise builds confidence; it also graciously accommodates and resolves complicated writing and publishing issues. Most importantly, it helps you to become more inclusive as you attract more global readers.

Researching and reviewing the work of other authors who have published books on similar topics as the one you will be writing, will also boost and reinforce your confidence about your writing responsibilities.

As you do your research, try to identify and connect with an organization or various readers who would immediately benefit in some way, from your writing. Your work should be solutions-oriented and focused to the specific types of readers.

While you may be inclined to mimic some techniques from your favorite authors as a new writer, you should be prepared to create your own unique approaches for your own work. It is important to create your own special branding. By no means, should you use your role model or competitor's information. As you identify your own writing style, you would be better positioned to capitalize on a very specific marketing niche.

After you identify what is most unusual about your writing, you should organize your content. It should include some specific personal "branding" around lifestyle or career issues and how it benefits your targeted readers.

Try to be as inclusive and as global as possible to engage culturally diverse readers. Even though you may want them to be culturally diverse, you should focus on retaining specific types of readers, such as educators versus entertainers. Remember that once your work is in print, it develops feet and wings of its own. You cannot control the far-away places that your work will travel. Identifying and targeting specific readers will alleviate any problems you may encounter with your competition later on relative to book sales, marketability and promotion.

Here are some randomly listed questions for you to consider when identifying your targeted readers:

1. Why am I writing this book?

2. What types of people should they be...professional, career minded, athletes, musicians, entertainers, women or clergy?

3. What should their age ranges be?

4. Why would they want to read my book and what would the information do for them?

5. Am I confident and proud about the content of my book?

NOTES

Some things I must do now are:

1. _____

2. _____

3. _____

4. _____

5. _____

6. _____

7. _____

8. _____

9. _____

10. _____

11. _____

12. _____

13. _____

14. _____

15. _____

Prioritizing Your Content

It is easy to prioritize your writing content when you use the PAM chart. This chart is a widely used writing strategy that helps to clear up any writer's block and organize your thoughts. It is a three-dimensional diagram of any shape that comprehensively links the three most important aspects of your writing content.

The letters "**PAM**" are used as an acronym that represents the **Purpose, Audience and Message** you want to send to your readers.   It also puts the specific topics of your writing content in the right perspective so that you can quickly identify what critical areas you might have overlooked or need to delete.

In the diagram below, the PAM is drawn and illustrated as three circles that are connected and labeled as follows:

The most effective way to use this chart is to jot down anything that comes into your mind about each topic within your writing content.   Each circle should contain any and all information related to the – purpose, audience or message.

Experience and best practice show that you should use the following three steps to maximize the PAM chart:

1. Never take time to initially analyze the words you jot down for the PAM chart.

2. Organize and prioritize your words in groups after you have jotted down every word you can think of that might be associated with your purpose, audience and message.

3. Create sentences from the most highly prioritized words in each category.

Remember that writing content or story lines have a beginning, middle and ending. Incorporate good grammar in your sentence construction and recognize your personal limitations. As identified, consider hiring an editor to assist you if you are unsure about your writing efforts at this stage of the writing process.

If you believe that you might be running out of ideas or content for your book, start creating a basic journal of the things that come to your mind. Then take the content from your journal to create another PAM chart with the same basic three steps. You should always incorporate the information from your journal with the content you already have to generate and increase your book content. This process allows you to identify and eliminate irrelevant information and to streamline your content to make it more succinct.

You will notice that your journaling process has added value when you use this process consistently. Be mindful however, that getting used to good journaling, may take a few weeks depending on your lifestyle and the time you have invested in your writing project.

As you become more proficient in your journaling, you may want to structure your information by topics and by dates. Your writing activity will allow you to clearly see where and how your efforts are being utilized. Most importantly journaling will keep you focused and on your writing schedule.

If you are concerned about the amount of information you have gathered for your book, and still have difficulty organizing your content into paragraphs for maximum impact, here are some techniques:

1. Create paragraphs by using your topic sentences.

2. Then elaborate on them.

3. Group everything you have written that is related to a specific topic into one paragraph.

4. Put each paragraph in sequential order for better readability.

5. Ask yourself questions about each specific topic or paragraph that begin with "who, what, where, why, how, when or if."

This 5th step will further generate more content and identify whether you have addressed the topic sufficiently and comprehensively.

You may want to consider prioritizing your paragraphs in chronological (ascending or descending), historical or incidental order. From this prioritized information, you will be able to further develop new topic sentences or lead sentences. This will embellish on what you have already written but in greater detail. You should continue to organize your content regularly as you add more content/ information. It will help you to quickly identify how much more you need to edit, rewrite or delete.

Should you feel a little overwhelmed by this process, take a break. Give yourself a couple of weeks to get the hang of the writing, and journaling processes. Taking a break from your writing provides a good opportunity to think more creatively and objectively for a masterful piece of work. However, the more you journal, the more you will find relevant book content. So use your topic sentences from your journal to jump start your writing.

An excellent time-saving and cost effective alternative strategy for you to consider if you are overwhelmed, would be to hire a professional writer or editor once you have all of your book-writing content. Be mindful that the more complicated or unclear your writing is, the more it will cost you to hire someone to rewrite or edit your work for you.

NOTES

Some things I must do now are:

1. _____

2. _____

3. _____

4. _____

5. _____

6. _____

7. _____

8. _____

9. _____

10. _____

11. _____

12. _____

13. _____

14. _____

15. _____

Autobiography Guidelines

More people seem to have a need to write autobiographies in the last decade. Maybe they felt some compulsion to have others benefit from their adverse life situations or because they have received some restitution for some injustices they have experienced. Some people might have survived unusual situations and are happy to share and empower others how to survive them or avoid them.

If you want to write about your life and are strongly convicted about doing so, pay close attention to the do's and don'ts of autobiographical writing. Focus and write about that significant something in your immediate or distant past so that you can take real ownership of it to embrace it with passion. You owe it to yourself and to your readers to have strong convictions about writing about your life.

Whatever the reasons might be to write your autobiography, the following information should provide some critical benchmarks for embarking on such a writing project. There are some realistic things to consider. You should ask yourself some very difficult and sometimes uncomfortable questions before embarking on this mission. A good yardstick for doing so is to ask yourself the following questions:

1. Would my mother-in-law, spouse, grandmother, grandchild, children or spiritual leader cringe in disgust

if they were to read about that part of my personal life?

2. Am I absolutely sure I want all of them to know that part of my life?

3. Would any of them grow or improve their lifestyles as a result of what I will share?

4. Can I live with that disclosure and how would others perceive me even though this disclosure may be in my distant past, I have changed, and am now a different person?

5. Would society value or respect me the same or treat me any better, once I tell my story?

6. After disclosure, would I need to relocate?

If all is well with you, then go for it!! It is best to write your story in chronological order or in five- year intervals depending on your circumstances, age or lifestyle. You may also want to consider specific events during the period in which you want to write. This could include your high school, college years or career experiences. You may even consider your personal relationships and the types of persons you seem to gravitate toward for all the wrong or right reasons. These areas tend to quickly jog your memory and fuel your creative writing style.

Courtship or your dating years, marriage(s). childbirth, accomplishments, birthdays, anniversaries, special events or hard times ought to give you great autobiographical content to jump start your writing. Only you can itemize those stages of your life in good taste. Hostility, a lot of negativity and profanity do not sell many books so watch how graphic or descriptive you become when reminiscing these times of your life.

If you believe you may go overboard with disclosure, bounce your anticipated content off with someone before you disclose it particularly if the thought of your past makes you angry and you may be inclined to use profanity or offensive expressions. It is important to recognize that other people besides your specifically targeted readers will read your book.

An autobiography is personal. Keep it honest and interesting. Be sure to maximize the PAM chart as was previously discussed as you chronicle the events in your life.

The following strategies and guidelines are listed to help you gather autobiographical book writing content:

1. List everything "interesting, mysterious, unique or controversial about your life that you can recall from your journal, diary or photographs. These may include activities, events (happy or sad), situations, personal thoughts or your general upbringing.

2. List all the lessons you have learned that were embarrassing, sad, happy or really empowering.

3. Be honest. Keep information consistent and alluring. Share what others would not know about you unless you chose to tell it.

4. Identify the most unique information you plan to share. No one really wants to read about what everybody in town does or has done.

5. Clearly state the purpose for writing your story. It should inform, motivate or persuade.

6. Incorporate those things about your life that will clearly

benefit your readers after they would have read your book.

7. Include some incidental humor whenever possible to humanize your story.

8. Describe some peculiar personal characteristics about yourself but keep them simple.

9. Create and maintain a consistent writing schedule, daily or weekly to stay focused on the theme of your book and its completion date.

10. Proofread, edit and re-read your book aloud and in a quiet place once you have completed your writing.

    This will help you to listen to the natural flow of your own speaking voice in your writing content.

11. Give your writing a title after you have made all of your necessary corrections from your final edit.

In case you are a little unsure about how to jumpstart your writing after reviewing these guidelines, use your imagination to envision a unisex pencil-drawn character of a human being was you, naked and void of any history. Treat it like an artist would a naked empty piece of canvass before he or she puts a splash of paint on it. Use that drawing to develop ideas and to paint a picture of your life with words. Use the limbs or body parts of that diagram as the different stages of your life so that your information would be comprehensive.

When you write your autobiography, make no excuses or apologies for doing so. Tell the unadulterated truth about yourself. It will help to give you a more objective perspective. Remember to lure your readers with some aspect of your life in your introduction of your book to keep them riveted to the

Below you will find some introspective questions that you may want to ask yourself so that you can really delve deeply into the "YOU" like no one else can. To expedite this process, I have taken the liberty to jog your thinking with some questions that will quickly identify interesting and unique autobiographical content for your book. Some of those questions are:

1. What are you obsessed about that you feel you need to share with the public?

2. What are your dreams or goals and would writing this impact them? Be specific by date and activity.

3. What have you accomplished or done that no one else has in spite of the odds that were against you?

4. What negatives have you overcome and are proud to comfortably share, inspire, motivate or encourage others to do?

5. Where were you born?

6. Are your parents alive and what are (were) they like?

7. Were your parents loving or strict?

8. Do you have siblings? How many are they? Do you like or get along well with them?

9. Where did you attend high school or college? Did you finish school and if so, from which school did you graduate?

10. If you did not graduate, what were some of the reasons?

11. Would you like to return to school and what would

you study if you had the opportunity?

12. Do you have any children and are they adults or of school age? Did they or do they challenge your parenting skills or lifestyle?

13. Are you proud of them or wish they were never born? If so, why? How happy did they make you?

14. Do you have a hobby and what is it?

15. What do you do for a living?

16. Do you believe in a Supreme Being (God) and if so, how does that belief influence or impact your lifestyle or decisions?

17. If you had the opportunity to live your live over again, what would you do differently?

I hope these questions have sufficiently jogged your memory so that you will be able to think of many more situations or questions for your autobiography. These questions and strategies will make your writing easier and challenge you to stay focused. The more you write and frame your writing within a certain thought process; you will better understand and appreciate how to release your thoughts.

It is not always a good practice to incorporate everything that you can think about or write in your journal, or on your PAM chart, into your autobiography. You may live to regret it. So be very selective of the content you choose to use.

For brainstorming purposes, give yourself permission to get truly liberated with questions so that you can maximize your vivid imagination to generate your book content. As you answer question #17 from the previous list of questions, try to identify three things that you would like to see materialized in the not-too-distant future.

During some of your introspection, it would also be ideal to identify and assess your personal relationship with God, the Supreme Being or whatever you may choose to call him. It will help you to better understand your own behavior as you reflect on some of the historical events or crises in your life. You should also be able to see very clearly, how that relationship guided or guides your life.

It is natural to initially feel a little intimidated or uncomfortable when you set out to write your autobiography. However, when you take the time to identify a step-by-step approach to do this, it should make your writing effortless. Remember if you describe the process of doing any activity in detail, it will sensitize you to overcoming any apprehension and maximize your organizational skills.

When you chronicle one of the personal experiences in your life, state what happened, where, how, when and why it happened. Remember to mention who was involved and if that experience could have been prevented or improved upon. Also describe how it was resolved, whether it was on a happy or sad note. If it were not resolved, you may want to take this opportunity to write your story without reservation, with strong conviction and a resolute emphasis on bringing it to some type of closure.

This very focused process will provide an excellent opportunity to cite specific examples of lessons learned in a very methodical manner. As you elaborate and chronicle those steps, you will quickly identify a title for your autobiography that would interest the readers you have targeted.

NOTES

Some things I must do now are:

1. _____

2. _____

3. _____

4. _____

5. _____

6. _____

7. _____

8. _____

9. _____

10. _____

11. _____

12. _____

13. _____

14. _____

15. _____

Guidelines for Children's Books

Writing children's books requires creativity and the capacity to shift your thinking from that of an adult to one of a child. If you have an interest in writing children's books, you may want to seriously consider the enumerated steps below. However, while other methodologies may be used, you will find this to be a practical reference or "cheat sheet" to expedite your book writing process. I recommend that you:

1. Identify subject and residence (location) of your book content.

2. Establish the age group of your targeted readers and their gender, male or female.

3. Create an environment or situation for your book content in which there would be some element of conflict, fear, fun, being lost, left alone, abandoned or rescued by a significant person or thing that is directly associated with the main character in your story.

4. Include or identify a happy, exciting ending or a clearly surprising resolution to your story.

5. Provide some fun-filled but practical activities with "childlike" sentiments throughout the story narrative.

6. Focus on the child as the reader by creating colorful imagery throughout your content.

7. Use a graphic artist to demonstrate and bring your imagery to life with bright and colorful pictures. These colors should always complement your story content for your specifically-targeted age readers.

8. Do not exceed 28 pages for this type of book.

9. Use concrete words to convey immediacy and to stimulate life-like imagery.

10. Avoid using "big" words. Coin similar sounding words for fun and story retention. Proofread, edit and re-read your story for simplicity and clarity.

NOTES

Some things I must do now are:

1. _____

2. _____

3. _____

4. _____

5. _____

6. _____

7. _____

8. _____

9. _____

10. _____

11. _____

12. _____

13. _____

14. _____

15. _____

Poetry Guidelines

Poetry has a remarkable way of leaving indelible impressions on its readers and hearers. Because people retain more of what they hear than what they see, choosing the right set of words in poetry is very, very important. The imprint of poetry may be a special message, musical rhythm of how the words flow or how the core content or story line is revealed.

Poetry writing is very delicate and requires some serious word crafting. Many people believe when they rhyme words to a musical tune, it should be considered as poetry. However, very rarely do such stringed-together words echo any semblance of poetic justice.

Poetic justice requires research, a vast knowledge volume of the subject and the application of technical writing strategies and guidelines. Essentially, a poet is required to paint pictures or images with words that can be retained to have some profound or residual impact on one's lifestyle, cultural or political situation.

It is important to note that the following guidelines may vary from author to author. However, there are some fundamental poetry-writing rules to follow that create good poetry because they significantly facilitate the writing efforts of beginning and creative poets. So after you do your research, you should:

1. Study the work of successful poets to understand their styles and how they craft images for retention.

2. Identify and use a declarative statement for your first stanza of your poem.

3. Write so that your syllables, words and stanzas flow naturally and comprehensively.

4. Start each stanza with a new idea and with a natural rhythm to retain readers' interest.

5. Write about life issues and situations but only give details when absolutely necessary.

6. Write about things or situations that are known to the general public as an alternative to writing about living things or human beings.

7. Create emotion when writing something personal or controversial.

8. Use a dictionary or thesaurus for metaphors, similes alliteration and so on, for clarity and impact.

9. Avoid malapropism (the misuse of words).

10. Use descriptive adjectives to create the sense of smell and taste. Use sound and the sense of touch to convey vibrant imagery.

11. Avoid rhyme in every sentence or stanza just for the sake of rhyming.

12. Use repetition wisely and intermittently for impact. Avoid clichés. They lack originality. Restructure clichés if you need to convey the same sentiment of their meaning.

13. Save your main message for the last stanza of your poem. It will have greater impact.

NOTES

Some things I must do now are:

1. _____

2. _____

3. _____

4. _____

5. _____

6. _____

7. _____

8. _____

9. _____

10. _____

11. _____

12. _____

13. _____

14. _____

15. _____

Writing Short Stories

There is an old adage which says, "Brevity is the source of wit." Writing short stories require that you convey your thoughts succinctly and as quickly as you can. So be sure that you are brief if you have a brilliant idea, a brainwave or two and want to write them down to be published. Decide whether you will write for some sentimental reason, information, persuasion or entertainment. Maybe you want to educate or motivate.

Whatever your reasons might be for writing a short story, consider using the following strategies before you begin writing to ensure that your work will be marketable:

1. Read several short stories that are of personal interest to you from different authors. Be sure to include some of the "classics" in your research.

2. Resist the temptation to steal an author's plot or ideas. It is illegal. It is also called plagiarism and it infringes on the author's copyright.

3. Use your own ideas so that you may preserve and dominate your own market niche.

4. Observe how the authors set plots, develop characters and write their dialogue.

5. Keep a notepad handy to jot down your ideas when

they come to you during the course of your day.

6. Maximize the use of the PAM chart to minimize or alleviate writer's block if it occurs.

7. Establish a beginning, middle and a dramatic ending to your short story.

8. Provide a topic sentence for each section that guides the readers' thoughts clearly.

9. Establish real life characters so that your readers can identify with them quickly.

10. Develop one to three main characters for quick comprehension to lure and keep readers' interests.

11. Keep your story "short." Do not exceed 30 pages. Remember the operant word for this type of writing is "short."

12. Write your story in the third person (he, she or they).

13. Lure your readers with a topic that is clearly universal, interesting, distracting, alarming, controversial or mysterious (like I did in the introduction of this book).

14. Avoid long character introductions or descriptions. Get straight to your plot.

15. Do more research than is required for your topic. It will give you vocabulary flexibility, more options for content, editing and rewriting as you craft your own style.

16. Find meaningful, fun-filled distraction if you get writer's block. It will help you to quickly refocus.

17. Share your story with friends, have them review it and solicit their constructive criticism.

18. Use all constructive criticism wisely and only as you deem appropriate as the author.

19. Maintain your author's integrity and purpose even with imposing suggestions or criticisms.

20. Review your content, proofread, edit, eliminate mechanical errors and submit a portion of or all of your content to the publisher.

21. Try to be disconnected emotionally from your manuscript after you submit it. This will help you to manage any rejection from the publisher.

NOTES

Some things I must do now are:

1. _____

2. _____

3. _____

4. _____

5. _____

6. _____

7. _____

8. _____

9. _____

10. _____

11. _____

12. _____

13. _____

14. _____

15. _____

Writing Activity Schedule

The only way to meet your identified writing deadline is to maintain a writing activity schedule. This schedule allows you to maintain some balance in your personal life which is essential to your writing process.

Once you have decided that you are ready to write, incorporate the guidelines below to stay better focused because it is very easy to become distracted without a writing schedule.

For your convenience:

1. Identify something that excites, upsets or obsesses you to write about it.

2. Establish a weekly commitment of time for writing based on your family, social and work life.

3. Find an inspiring environment in which to write. One that has or reminds you of sunshine, a beautiful fall or spring day. A happy occasion or location would also be a good place to start.

4. If you do not have a window to glance at or through when you sit down to write, try to have the outdoors peak through your selected place to write. You may also want to find a picture, painting or poster that will conjure up an atmosphere of the outdoors so that

your mind will be free to escape and wander when you are stuck for a word or two. Remember there is so much to see outdoors that it will allow your imagination to roam freely when writer's block passes your way.

5. Visit bookstores or the library in your neighborhood to review some opening sentences of books like the one you want to write. Absorb as much of that information to create your unique style and content.

6. Divide the contents of each book you review into sections to learn how you can structure your chapters or define the layout of your book.

7. Create topic sentences for your chapters to craft an outline or the table of contents for your book.

8. Identify timelines by dates to complete each chapter of your book.

9. Create and post a schedule of your writing activity in a prominent place so that you can stay closely connected to the reality of your writing objective.

   a. **For fiction:** Identify and detail the characters in your book by function. You should describe them by the roles they will play and how they should look. Prepare this just like you would write a job description.

   b. Develop your plot, establish and assign the roles of all of your characters at the same time.

   c. Identify and maintain three characters (persons) in your book by specific actions and purpose for credibility.

d. Try to become the characters you create so that you can write them with clarity and emotion for greater impact.

e. Structure how the characters will interact with the protagonist (main character).

10. Remember to format your book content with a beginning, middle and ending.

11. Keep a writing pad or tape recorder with or close to you so that you can easily speak or write down ideas or "brain waves" as they tend to come when you least expect.

12. Write your ideas in longhand to minimize editing and to quickly remember them since Shorthand has a tendency to get stale and illegible when not transcribed immediately. It is a strong possibility that you would forget what you have written if you use shorthand.

13. Write consistently. Purchase and use the *Naturally Speaking Software* if you have difficulty typing your ideas as quickly as they come into your mind. (With this software, everything you speak will be typed for you).

14. Research "published journals" online for factual details and use Harper's Magazine for historical data.

15. Write with vivid imagination, conviction, authority and passion.

16. Let your daily subconscious thoughts provoke your creativity with surprises. Use that spontaneity wisely to spark and retain your readers' interest.

17. Take full responsibility for maximizing your vocabulary.

18. Use active verbs and do not be afraid to capitalize on adjectives. They paint wonderful pictures.

19. Organize your thoughts and chapters carefully so that they are clear and easy to read for maximum impact.

20. Read books on food and gardening to keep "word" descriptions alive and succinct.

21. Use concrete words for quick imagery and retention.

22. Take a 2-day break each week from writing to refresh your enthusiasm and let your creative writing "juices" to flow.

23. Give your book a generic title and start editing to streamline your book content.

24. Ask yourself all possible questions about your book for content sufficiency as you proofread and edit.

25. Review and edit your book again for comprehension, impact and readability. This will ensure that you have addressed your intended subject adequately and the way in which you intended.

26. Look for, and eliminate excessive punctuation, awkward word structures and clichés.

27. Read your book content aloud or into a tape recorder as you listen for careless mistakes.

28. Do your spell check and have another person read it for an objective perspective on marketability.

After you have completed all of your writing and proofreading activities, draft a one-page summary of your manuscript describing your book content. Create a one-page bio of yourself. Select and copy the first 50 pages of your book (or your entire manuscript) to send to the publisher. Write a query letter to the publisher, attach and mail everything to the publisher.

Now that you have mailed your manuscript to the publisher, inform everyone you know by Email (because it's the most cost-effective and less time-consuming) to let them know about your book.

Do the same with local bookstores after you have received confirmation from your publisher about the expected date your book will be in print. Ask the bookstore or sales manager to carry your book in their stores. Request a book signing date in their stores. It will save you hundreds of marketing and promotion dollars.

NOTES

Some things I must do now are:

1. _____

2. _____

3. _____

4. _____

5. _____

6. _____

7. _____

8. _____

9. _____

10. _____

11. _____

12. _____

13. _____

14. _____

15. _____

Query Letters

A query letter is one of fact finding that you will send to a publisher. You should include basic information about your writing project in your query letters to publishers that is similar to any letter you will write requesting something specific from a company or organization.

Query letters should include your full name, (or pen name), a reliable current address, email address and your current phone number. Generally, an author usually wants to find out his or her publication costs, the deadline dates for their books to be in print, book delivery to bookstores, and general publicity venue exposure to include: marketing and promotional opportunities, strategies and advertising options.

Your letter should be cordial and precise with the traditional salutation, Dear Publisher (or use a name if available). The following essential book information to include in your letter to the publisher should be:

1. Your book title and the number of pages in your book.

2. A summary of your book in 50 words or less.

3. The reason you chose the title or topic of your book.

4. A description of the genre, fiction or non-fiction.

5. Your targeted readers such as their ages, gender, lifestyles, occupations or hobbies.

6. The geographic location of your targeted readers whether they live globally or regionally.

7. A request or explanation of what the publisher has to offer you and what your next steps should be after submitting your work.

8. A closing,"Thank you," your name and title as the author.

You will need to be reconciled to disclosing a long-standing home address in lieu of a Post Office Box number because the publisher's response time may take longer than you expect. A street address is usually preferred for direct billing and follow up correspondence from the publisher.

Always let the publishers know whether such disclosure of a specially-targeted city or state would bias and/or negatively impact your book sales from region to region. This clarification is necessary only if you opt to give a post office box number instead of a street address as contact information.

Be sure to "sell" your book to the publisher. Give the publisher every good reason why readers would be interested in purchasing your book. Lastly, request a possible date or time frame in which you may expect to get a response from them.

NOTES

Some things I must do now are:

1. _____

2. _____

3. _____

4. _____

5. _____

6. _____

7. _____

8. _____

9. _____

10. _____

11. _____

12. _____

13. _____

14. _____

15. _____

Identifying Publishers

There are many local publishers in your region that provide cost-effective publishing options for authors who want to self publish. Your budget, writing purpose and market niche will help you to determine your choice for selecting a publishing company. Identifying and selecting a publisher however, is a very personal matter.

Generally, people who self-publish want to identify publishers based upon the urgency to have their books in print and the benefit packages that some publishers offer to promote their books.

Publishers' packages vary. It is for this reason that authors have to personally research and identify publishers which meet their unique needs or hire someone to do that for them. A major consideration for identifying publishers is due to the rapidly changing technology for books on demand.

It is a good practice to get references from other published authors to identify the most appropriate publisher for your work and with your particular preferences.

It is for this reason no publisher is recommended besides the one who publishes this book.

NOTES

Some Things I must do now are:

1. _____
2. _____
3. _____
4. _____
5. _____
6. _____
7. _____
8. _____
9. _____
10. _____
11. _____
12. _____
13. _____
14. _____
15. _____

Book Contracts and Publishers

Like any business contract, book contracts specify the arrangement between two people, the publisher and the author. A book contract protects either party and should at least, clearly detail the following things:

- Due date for a manuscript

- Contract limitations

- Book publication date

- Sale price for your book

- Printing/publication deposit

- Advance (money) an author receives

- Book royalties an author receives

Some contracts have other specific stipulations and agreements. However, it is very important to read the "fine print" or have an attorney or someone with a good understanding of contracts, review the aspects of the contract that might be unclear.

Because this book is written for the sole purpose of jump starting your creativity and writing style for self-publishing, information on this topic is limited. The best practice is to research specific information on global book contracts as you get closer to the completion of your book.

NOTES

Some things I must do now are:

1. _____
2. _____
3. _____
4. _____
5. _____
6. _____
7. _____
8. _____
9. _____
10. _____
11. _____
12. _____
13. _____
14. _____
15. _____

Publicity Strategies

The public relations, marketing and promotions require tenacity. A strong commitment to your writing effort will propel you to identify diverse venues for promoting your book. Some of the strategies that facilitate best practices for book promotions will require that you:

1. Submit as much information as you can about your book to bookstores, magazine and newspaper editors.

2. Become very specific about your publicity requests and your promotional preferences.

3. Understand the difference between advertising and publicity.

4. Call all media personnel to promote your work until they answer your questions sufficiently.

5. Return all interested media personnel calls in a timely manner.

6. Explore all media resources and be persistent in getting positive publicity for your work.

7. Become familiar with "lead times" for the print media. Some monthly magazines have a four-month lead time for promotions and advertising if you want your work profiled in print.

8. Do your homework by becoming familiar with media outlets to which you are pitching.

9. Have high-resolution 300 dpi or higher photos of yourself, your book cover, and artwork readily available for print promotions.

10. Prepare press releases for all newspapers, local radio and TV stations.

11. Call electronic media for live or recorded interviews and offer a complimentary copy of your book to specific listeners for promotional purposes.

12. Take advantage of special local and national events and attend them to promote your book.

13. Remember to stay positive while you wait to hear from publishers.

Publicity and promotions for your book can be very time-consuming and hectic for any author. That is why many authors hire someone to promote and sell their books for them. If you fail to keep your book in the public's eye, it will become an old dust-collector, sitting on a shelf wishing someone would pick it up.

NOTES

Some things I must do now are:

1. _____

2. _____

3. _____

4. _____

5. _____

6. _____

7. _____

8. _____

9. _____

10. _____

11. _____

12. _____

13. _____

14. _____

15. _____

Conclusion

I trust that these practical illustrations and guidelines boosted your confidence to complete your writing project with clarity and impact. First-time or seasoned writers should find these strategies, guidelines, the pros and cons of writing very easy to use as they research and gather writing content.

The bulleted guidelines should create the platform for your story ideas. These practical nuggets of information ought to have clarified and separated the difference between wishful thinking and writing with the specific purpose to get published.

I hope you live your dream as a published author in the not-too-distant future. Most importantly, remember to release your wild imagination and expand your vocabulary to describe what you feel, see and want to convey in writing. If needed, model the introductory chapter, His Lips Excite Me.

As you think about the story line in the introduction chapter, His Lips Excite Me, I hope that you will at least get a chuckle out of it and remember my intent was to lure you into reading some very valuable information on writing skills. I sincerely hope that you understood the risk that I took with this title. Remember to value your own bold and creative expression when you write.

I know that the information shared has derailed your first impression and I hope that you will grow from the lesson shared. As you set out to research information for your writing project, be diligent by getting appropriate core content. Follow the guidelines and writing structures for your specific writing project. Relax and let your words take flight with your creative writing style. Organize your content with the practical strategies to revive your spirit when writer's block shows up. Remember that your unique style identifies your personal branding. Take the risk. You will have fun and grow from it.

I hope that you will use and carry this sourcebook as a quick reference for your writing projects. Even though I did not disclose whose lips excite me, for whatever it was worth, I hope this non-disclosure has been a meaningful exercise in creative writing.

My imagination and risky creativity should have stimulated or provoked your presumptive thought process for the greater good. I also hope that this approach to creative writing has broadened your writing perspective. So, write with conviction and passion so that others will be empowered!

As you travel down the Self-publishing Highway, remember to turn right and cruise along Imagination Lane. Stop at the Creative Crosswalk; use the guidelines and strategies to navigate your specific writing destination. At the intersection of Content Insufficiency, Writer's Block, Confused Organization and Word Malfunction, pull over and park on the Sourcebook Sidewalk. Identify your location, then make a quick U-turn on Brainstorm Boulevard to navigate your way back to Creative Intersection. Make a quick right turn on Risk Avenue where you will find your publishing destination and **His Lips Will Excite You**! Now go and get self-published.

NOTES

The summary of my <u>previous</u> notes include the following topic sentences:

1. _____

2. _____

3. _____

4. _____

5. _____

6. _____

7. _____

8. _____

9. _____

10. _____

11. _____

12. _____

13. _____

14. _____

15. _____

References and Resources

The following list of books is provided to support the guidelines and strategies in this sourcebook. It is specifically designed to document some research which is shared but shared in a simplistic way, void of the typical or technical bibliographic structures and punctuation illustrated in traditional books.

1. The Marshall Plan for Getting Your Novel Published by Evan Marshall.

2. The Complete Guide to Self Publishing by Tom and Marilyn Ross.

3. Get Your First Book Published by Jason Shinder.

4. An Insider's Guide to Getting Your Book the Attention It Deserves by Jacqueline Deval.

5. The Complete Guide to Self Publishing by Ross & Ross.

6. Publicize Your Book by Jacqueline Deval.

7. The Complete Handbook of Novel Writing by Meg Leder, and Jack Heffron.

8. Facts in a Flash by Ellen Metter.

9. Careers for Your Characters by Raymond Obstfeld and Franz Neumann.

10. Fiction Writer's Brainstormer by James V. Smith, Jr.

Suggested Writing Software

- Naturally Speaking Software for Word Processing

- Novel Writing Software: New Novelist version 2.0

- Poetry Software: Masterwriter